INTRO

Dear readers, in this book you are going to learn about the Mother of Jesus and Her visits to different parts of the world.

Her visits were to children just like you. Some were shepherds of sheep, others students at school, and all were loving followers of Jesus.

In each of Her visits, Mother Mary introduced Herself in a different way. She gave special names to describe Herself. She used these names to tell us about the reason for Her visit.

For instance, in one place, She called Herself 'The Lady of the Rosary' to show the importance of praying the Holy Rosary. In another place, she called herself 'Queen of Peace' to teach us about living in God's peace.

Each chapter will tell us about one of Mother Mary's visits. First, we will learn about who She visited, 'The Messengers'. Then, we will learn about Her name and appearance during this visit, 'The Mother'. Finally, we will learn about Her special instructions to the children She visited, 'The Message'.

As you read these stories, pray that the Holy Mother may speak to your heart and inspire you to live according to Her and Her Son's Gospel message of love.

ONE: FATIMA
THE MESSENGERS OF FATIMA

Once upon a time, in a small village called Fatima, nestled among beautiful mountains in Portugal, three special children had an extraordinary experience. It was the year 1917, a time when a great war was causing turmoil around the world. But amidst the chaos, something magical was about to unfold.

The village of Fatima was filled with a deep faith in the Catholic religion, and it played an important part in the lives of everyone there. For Lucia, who was nine years old, and her cousins Jacinta, who was six, and Francisco, who was seven, their daily routine involved tending their family's sheep and finding joy in praying the rosary.

Lucia was a remarkable child with bright, twinkling eyes and a heart full of love. She had a captivating personality and possessed a special gift of leadership. Other children in the village looked up to her with trust and affection. Lucia had an incredible memory, which allowed her to learn about the teachings of the faith, and she even made her First Communion and Confession when she was just six years old. She was like a guiding light for her beloved cousins, Francisco and Jacinta, always there to support and help them.

And so, the stage was set for a holy adventure that would forever change the lives of these three brave children. Little did they know that they were about to witness something truly extraordinary and receive a divine message that would touch the hearts of people all over the world.

THE MOTHER: THE LADY OF THE ROSARY

One sunny day, as Lucia, Francisco, and Jacinta were looking after their family's sheep in the peaceful fields, something truly magical occurred. A magnificent lady dressed all in white, shining brighter than the sun itself, appeared before their very eyes. The children couldn't believe what they were seeing!

With a gentle smile, the radiant lady spoke to them, saying, "I am the Lady of the Rosary." It was no ordinary lady but the Mother of God Herself who stood before them. This encounter was just the beginning of an extraordinary series of events that would unfold over the months to come.

Each month, on the 13th day, the Lady would return to visit the children. From May to October in the year 1917, She would grace them with Her presence, sharing special messages and filling their hearts with hope and love. It was a secret and sacred bond between the children and the Lady, which they treasured dearly.

Then came the momentous month of October. The Lady told the children that this would be Her final visit. Excitement filled the air as the children eagerly awaited the promised sign that would prove to the world that the Lady had truly appeared before them.

THE GREAT MIRACLE OF THE SUN

On that miraculous day, nearly 70,000 people, from far and wide, gathered in the fields despite the heavy rain and mud. They had faith in their hearts and hope in their eyes. And then, the extraordinary happened. The clouds parted, and the sun emerged, shining brilliantly like a disk of white fire.

The sun began to dance in the sky, spinning and twirling with such joy and grace. It painted the world with a spectacular display of colors that reflected on the amazed faces of the crowd. As the miracle unfolded, something incredible occurred – the rain-soaked clothes of the people miraculously dried, as if touched by the Lady's heavenly hand.

This breathtaking event became known as "The Miracle of the Sun. " It was a powerful sign that touched the hearts of all who witnessed it. News of the miracle spread far and wide, inspiring people to believe in heaven's messages, have faith, and pray with devotion to the Lady of the Rosary.

THE MESSAGE OF FATIMA

The Lady of the Rosary said these words to the children:
"Say the Rosary every day to bring peace to the world and the end of the war."

"He (Jesus) wishes to establish the devotion to My Immaculate Heart throughout the world. I promise salvation to whoever embraces it; these souls will be dear to God, like flowers put by Me to adorn his throne."

"Pray, pray very much, and make sacrifices for sinners; for many souls go to hell, because there are none to sacrifice themselves and pray for them...If what I say to you is done, many souls will be saved and there will be peace."

"He (God) is about to punish the world for its crimes, by means of war, famine, and persecutions of the Church and of the Holy Father."

"To prevent this, I shall come to ask for the consecration of Russia to my Immaculate Heart, and the Communion of Reparation on the First Saturdays. If my requests are heeded, Russia will be converted, and there will be peace; if not, she will spread her errors throughout the world, causing wars and persecutions of the Church. The good will be martyred, the Holy Father will have much to suffer, various nations will be annihilated. In the end, my Immaculate Heart will triumph."

TWO: KIBEHO
THE MESSENGERS OF KIBEHO

Once upon a time, in a small town called Kibeho, in the beautiful land of Rwanda, something astonishing happened. It was a time when tensions were running high, and a war was looming over the land. But amidst all the worries and fears, a ray of hope appeared.

In Kibeho, there was a special school called Kibeho College, where three remarkable girls named Alphonsine, Nathalie, and Marie Claire were students. Alphonsine was seventeen years old, Nathalie was eighteen, and Marie Claire was twenty-one. They were ordinary girls with big hearts and dreams.

One fateful day, on November 28, 1981, at exactly 12:35 p.m., the most amazing thing happened. The Blessed Virgin Mary, the Mother of Jesus, appeared before one of these three girls. Later She would appear to the others.

Our Lady first appeared to Alphonsine in the school's dining room. Imagine Alphonsine's surprise when She heard a gentle voice calling Her name. "My daughter," the voice said. Alphonsine, curious and a little nervous, replied, "Here I am. Who are you?"

"I am the Mother of the Word," the Heavenly Mother replied with warmth. "In your faith, what do you desire?" Alphonsine, filled with love for God and His Mother, replied, "I love God and His Mother, who gave us the Child who redeemed us."

Hearing Alphonsine's sincere words, Mother Mary smiled. She had come to bring comfort and hope to the girls during these troubled times. "I have come to calm you," She said, "because I have heard your prayers. But I would also like your friends to have faith, as they do not believe strongly enough." From that day forward, the lives of Alphonsine, Nathalie, and Marie Claire were forever changed.

THE MOTHER: THE MOTHER OF THE WORD

In the small town of Kibeho, a place filled with beautiful flowers and towering trees, this Heavenly Mother introduced Herself as the "Mother of the Word," which meant in the Rwandan language the "Mother of God."

The Heavenly Mother was like no other. She had a radiant smile that could light up the entire sky. She wore a stunning seamless white dress and a delicate white veil that gently rested on Her head. With Her hands clasped together over Her heart. She held a beautiful Rosary of the Seven Sorrows.

As the girls continued to see these visions, they noticed that the Heavenly Mother stood in the midst of a breathtaking field of flowers. Each flower represented a soul that was filled with God's grace and love. It was a truly inspiring sight!

But along with the beauty and love, the Heavenly Mother also showed the girls some difficult and scary images. She wanted to teach them important lessons about love, compassion, and the consequences of hate and violence. She showed them images of Heaven, Hell, and Purgatory, as well as the story of Jesus' suffering, so they could understand the power of forgiveness and kindness.

A HEARTBREAKING VISION

One of the visions was especially heartbreaking. The girls saw images of future people hurting each other, rivers of blood, and fires that seemed to never end. It was a glimpse into a dark time in Rwanda's history, when many innocent people lost their lives in a terrible civil war. Thousands of people were affected, and it was a painful chapter in the country's story.

Even the town of Kibeho, where the girls lived and saw these amazing visions, was not spared from the horrors. There were two terrible massacres that took place there, causing immense sadness and grief. The people in the church and the students from the college where the girls attended were among those who tragically lost their lives.

But through all the sorrow and pain, the messages of the Heavenly Mother remained. She wanted to remind everyone that love, compassion, and faith are stronger than any darkness in the world. She wanted the girls and all the children of Rwanda to hold on to hope and strive for a future filled with peace, forgiveness and understanding.

THE MESSAGE OF KIBEHO

'The Mother of the Word' said to the children of Kibeho:
"Since you saw these three categories (Heaven, Hell and Purgatory), it is my hope now that you will do your best to attract people to the right path. Moreover, I showed them to you so you can learn that the best life is to come after man leaves the earth. And truly, to live comfortably in this life without caring about the Creator and His Will, is a waste of time."

"Repent, repent, repent! When I tell you this, I speak also to all the others. Men of our times have emptied each thing of its true meaning. They commit faults and don't recognize that they did wrong. Meditate about the Passion of Jesus, and on the deep Sorrows of His Mother. Recite the Rosary every day, and also the Rosary of the Seven Sorrows of Mary, to obtain the favor of repentance."

"The path to Heaven always leads through suffering. A true child of Mary cannot be separated from suffering."

"Pray, pray, pray! Do not worry about those who say you waste your time, and you are lazy. You who pray will have the reward. You will be happy! Follow the Gospel of my Son, saddened by those who despise Him. My Son suffered. They chased and struck Him. But this did not prevent Him being the King of Heaven and Earth."

One must recite the Rosary every day,
and also the Rosary of the Seven Sorrows of Mary,
to obtain the favour of repentence.

-Our Lady of Kabeho

THREE: MEDJUGORJE
THE MESSENGERS OF MEDJUGORJE

Once, in a small village called Medjugorje, in Bosnia-Herzegovina, there were six teenagers enjoying their beautiful natural surroundings. It was a sunny afternoon in Europe, and the date was June 24, 1981, which was the special day of the feast of St. John the Baptist.

These teenagers, whose names were Ivanka, Mirjana, Vicka, Ivan, Marija, and the young Jakov, were between the ages of twelve and twenty. Little did they know that this day would be like no other they had ever experienced.

As they walked along the hillside, something incredible happened!

Up in the sky, they saw a radiant figure shining brightly. It was a young woman holding a child in her arms, and she looked so beautiful and filled with light. It was none other than the Virgin Mary Herself!

But, oh dear, the teenagers were frightened by this extraordinary sight and quickly ran away. When they reached their homes, they gathered the courage to tell their families what they had seen. However, the adults found it hard to believe their amazing tale.

The following day, word spread, and many people came to the hill, now known as Apparition Hill, hoping to catch a glimpse of the Lady. And She appeared again! The six children felt an urging in their hearts, as if the Lady was encouraging them to climb to the top of the hill.

With excitement and curiosity, the children followed the Lady and swiftly made their way up the hill. When they reached the summit, to their astonishment, there She was once more, waiting for them. The Lady spoke to them kindly and made a promise that she would return again.

THE HOLY MOTHER RETURNS

On the third day, more than a thousand people gathered on the hill, hoping to witness the miraculous event. One of the children, filled with both doubt and wonder, decided to test the Lady. They threw some holy water towards Her to see if she truly was the Virgin Mary. And you know what? The Lady smiled warmly and confirmed that it was indeed the Holy Mother of Jesus.

She spoke to the children about the importance of peace and discovering a connection with God. Her words touched the hearts of everyone who listened. News of this extraordinary happening quickly spread across the world, attracting visitors from every corner.

Even to this day, people from all walks of life come to Medjugorje to visit the place where the Virgin Mary appeared and still continues to appear. It has become a place of pilgrimage, where people seek solace, hope, and faith.

THE MOTHER: THE QUEEN OF PEACE

The first thing Our Lady of Medjugorje spoke about was peace. She invited everyone to seek inner and spiritual peace. On the third day of her visits, She said, "Peace, peace, peace! Be reconciled! Only peace. Make your peace with God and among yourselves. For that, it is necessary to believe, to pray, to fast, and to go to Confession."

Our Lady had a special name for these visits to Medjugorje. She called Herself "The Queen of Peace," because She wanted to bring peace to everyone's hearts and minds. One day, on a Monday on August 24, 1981, something amazing happened. Many people in Medjugorje looked up at the sky and saw the word "MIR" written in fiery letters on top of a mountain called Mount Krizevac. Do you know what "MIR" means? It means "peace" in Croatian, the language spoken in that village.

One of the children who saw Our Lady, named Vicka, described Her in a very special way. She said Our Lady looked like a wonderful girl, about twenty years old, with beautiful blue eyes and black wavy hair. She wore a long dress and a light veil on Her head. Vicka said that Our Lady's face was shaped like an oval and She had pink lips and cheekbones. Our Lady always had a sweet smile that made everyone feel loved.

Something magical about Our Lady was that She floated on a cloud, and her feet were covered by Her dress. She wore a crown on Her head made of twelve stars, representing the twelve tribes of Israel, the twelve Apostles and Mary's twelve great virtues. The crown showed how special and important She was. She is a Queen of Hearts!

THE MESSAGE OF MEDJUGORJE

The Blessed Mother's messages are powerful weapons against the enemy: We may defeat evil by living the five main messages or **five stones** of Our Lady:

1. Pray the Rosary with our Heart Daily!- "Only in this way will you comprehend that your life is empty without prayer. You will discover the meaning of your life when you discover God in prayer." (July 25, 1997)

2. Fast Twice Every Week!- "Through fasting and prayer one can stop wars, one can suspend the laws of nature."
"And to fast strictly on Wednesdays and Fridays…" (August 14, 1984)

3. Holy Confession Every Month!- "There is no one on earth who does not need to go to confession at least once a month,"
"…You cannot, little children, realize peace if you are not at peace with Jesus. Therefore, I invite you to confession so Jesus may be your truth and peace." (January 25, 1995)

4. Receive the Eucharist Every Sunday!- "Holy Mass is the greatest prayer; it is the most sacred time of your life!" "Go to church in order to have a personal encounter with God. Those who go only out of habit or to see their friends are unbelievers." (Mirjana,1982) "Fall in love with the Most Holy Sacrament of the altar! Adore Him, little children, in your parishes." (Sept. 25, 1995)

5. Read the Bible Daily!- "Dear Children, you have forgotten the Bible! Put the Bible in a visible place in your homes. Read several verses each day and put these verses into practice during your day. Let the people who come into your homes be able to see the Bible and read passages from it with you. In that way, you will be able to talk about God together."

24

Holy Rosary

Fasting

Confession

Eucharist

Bible

FOUR: GARABANDAL
THE MESSENGERS OF GARABANDAL

Many years ago, in a small village called San Sebastian de Garabandal, there were four girls who loved to play in the fields. Their names were Conchita, Loli, Jacinta, and Maria Cruz. They were all very simple and kind-hearted girls, living in a poor rural area nestled on the slopes of the Cantabrian mountains in Spain.

One sunny Sunday evening, on June 18, 1961, something heavenly happened. As the girls were playing and enjoying some delicious apples, they heard a strange sound, like thunder rolling through the sky. They looked at each other in surprise. The mysterious thunder sounded like a voice from God.

Conchita, holding an apple in her hand, said, "Oh no! We just ate the stolen apples. The devil must be happy now, and our guardian angels must be sad." The girls wanted to make their angels happy again, so Conchita came up with an idea. She said, "Let's throw stones at the devil to show our love for the angels!"

As they were throwing stones, incredibly, a beautiful figure suddenly appeared before Conchita, who was twelve years old. The figure was surrounded by a gentle radiance that didn't hurt her eyes. The figure was in the sky, and Conchita's head fell back and her eyes were fixed upwards. She was feeling a sense of awe and wonder. The other girls, Jacinta, Loli, and Maria Cruz, who were eleven years old, saw Conchita in this state and thought something was wrong. But before they could call for help, the same thing happened to them too!

They all looked up in the direction Conchita was staring, and to their amazement, they saw the angel too! The angel stood there silently, and the girls felt a deep sense of peace and joy in his presence. This incredible vision lasted for half an hour, without a single word spoken. Little did they know that this silent encounter marked the beginning of one of the most extraordinary stories in human history, as proclaimed by Pope Paul VI.

THE MOTHER: THE LADY OF MOUNT CARMEL

On July 1st, the angel appeared to the four girls and said that the Blessed Virgin Mary Herself would come to see them the very next day! The following day, just after 6 p.m., the girls gathered on a rocky lane, eagerly waiting for the arrival of the Virgin Mary. Suddenly, there She was, surrounded by a beautiful light that made everything glow. Standing on either side of Her were two angels, and one of them was the same angel they had been seeing before. They now knew him as St. Michael, a powerful and loving angel.

The Blessed Mary was a vision of beauty. She wore a white robe with delicate flower patterns and a blue mantle. On Her head, She had a crown adorned with twelve golden stars. In Her hand, She held a large brown Scapular, which looked like the Scapular of Mount Carmel.

Mary's long, dark hair flowed down to Her waist, and it was parted in the middle. Her face was incredibly lovely, with a dainty nose, a pretty mouth, and slightly full lips. She looked as young and radiant as a seventeen-year-old girl. When She spoke, Her voice was sweet and pure, unlike any other voice the girls had ever heard. It was like listening to a heavenly melody.

Mary spoke to the girls with love and warmth, just like a caring mother talking to Her beloved daughters. She listened attentively to their simple questions and little stories, making them feel cherished and important.
"My dear children," Mary said, "I am the Lady of Mount Carmel! I have come for all my children." Her words carried a message of love and hope, reaching out to everyone who believes in Her.

THE MESSAGE OF GARABANDAL

Our Lady foretold three momentous events that would occur:

A Worldwide Warning & A Miraculous Sign

The Blessed Virgin revealed: There will be a Warning that will "draw the good closer to God and warn the wicked that the end of time is coming." The Warning will be seen and experienced by everyone everywhere. Each person will find himself alone with his conscience before God, able to know all his sins and what his sins have caused. Hopefully, this could influence a worldwide "purification" before The Miracle happens. The Miracle would follow the Warning within a year.

The Miracle will be a supernatural public display in the area of the pines, "that will prove and manifest God's love to us in a most outstanding way." It will be visible to all in the village and surrounding areas. The sick that will be present shall be cured; the sinners present will all be converted. A sign of The Miracle will remain forever at the pines – but cannot be touched – just photographed.

A Chastisement

Our Lady: "We must make many sacrifices, perform penance, and visit the Blessed Sacrament frequently. But first, we must lead good lives. If we do not, a chastisement will befall us. The cup is already filling up, and if the people do not change, a very great chastisement will come upon us." (July 4, 1961)

Later she said: "Before, the cup was filling up. Now, it is flowing over. Many cardinals, many bishops, and many priests are on the road to perdition – and are taking many souls with them.

Less and less importance is being given to the Eucharist. You should turn the wrath of God away from yourselves by your efforts. If you ask His forgiveness with sincere hearts, He will pardon you. I, your mother, through the intercession of St. Michael the Archangel, ask you to amend your lives. You are now receiving the last warnings..."
(June 18, 1965)

FIVE: AKITA
THE MESSENGER OF AKITA

Several decades ago in Japan, there was a kind and devoted sister named Agnes Sasagawa. She had always felt a special calling from God and knew from a young age that she wanted to dedicate her life to serving Him. So, she joined the Institute of the Handmaids of the Holy Eucharist and became a nun.

Sister Agnes had many important responsibilities as a sister. She spent time praying and adoring God, helping others in need, and doing various tasks to assist her community.

One day, something incredible happened to Sister Agnes. It was June 12, 1973, and she was praying in the chapel of her convent. Suddenly, she saw a beautiful and mysterious light shining from the tabernacle, where the Blessed Sacrament was kept. It was like nothing she had ever seen before!

But that wasn't the end. Two days later, on June 14, Sister Agnes and her fellow sisters were gathered in prayer before the Blessed Sacrament. As they prayed, a mysterious red light appeared, filling the room with a sense of wonder and joy. Sister Agnes knew in her heart that something extraordinary was about to happen.

The next day, she had her first vision, Sister Agnes saw heavenly beings worshiping the Eucharist. It was a sight that filled her with awe and reminded her of the real presence of Christ in the Eucharist. From that day, Sister Agnes continued to receive messages from her guardian angel.

Then, on July 6, 1973, something truly miraculous occurred. Sister Agnes saw the wooden statue of the Virgin Mary in her chapel come to life and speak to her. It was a moment filled with love and grace, and Sister Agnes knew that the Blessed Mother was truly present with her.

It's interesting to note that the name "Agnes" means lamb in Latin. And just like a lamb, Sister Agnes experienced a miracle. During these extraordinary events, she was healed of her deafness. It was a miracle that showed the world the truth and authenticity of the visits from Our Lady.

THE MOTHER: THE LADY OF ALL NATIONS

As Sister Agnes knelt in prayer, in her chapel on the 28th of July, she looked up and saw a beautiful cloud of angels surrounding the altar. It was a breathtaking sight! Suddenly, she felt a strange sensation in her left palm. When she opened her hand, she couldn't believe her eyes. There, right in the center of her palm, was a mark that looked like a cross. It was like it had been engraved on her skin, and it even had blood coming from it. It was a very unusual and miraculous mark, known as the wound of stigmata.

But something even more astonishing happened. Sister Agnes looked over at the statue of the Virgin Mary, called 'Our Lady of All Nations', that stood in the chapel. And guess what? The statue had the same cross-like wound in the palm of its little hand, just like Sister Agnes. Blood was also flowing from the statue's wound. It was a moment that was filled with wonder and amazement.

Then, on a special day in July, Sister Agnes was led to the chapel by her guardian angel. She knelt before the tabernacle, feeling a deep sense of love and adoration. As she approached the statue of the Virgin Mary and looked at the wound on Her hand, something incredible happened. A sweet voice, like music, came from the statue. Sister Agnes, who was usually deaf, could hear the voice clearly. It was the first message she received, and it was truly miraculous!

The miracles continued to happen. Some sisters discovered drops of blood flowing from the statue's right hand, and it seemed like the statue was even sweating from its forehead and neck. It was as if the statue itself was alive and experiencing the love and pain of the world.

Months passed, and in August and October of the same year, Sister Agnes received two more messages from the Virgin Mary. The messages were warnings from heaven asking people to repent and turn away from sin. Sister Agnes cherished each word and held them close to her heart.

THE MESSAGE OF AKITA

The First Message of Our Lady- "Pray in reparation for the sins of men…let us pray it together: 'Most Sacred Heart of Jesus, truly present in Holy Eucharist, I consecrate my body and soul to be entirely one with Your Heart, being sacrificed at every instant on all the altars of the world and giving praise to the Father pleading for the coming of His Kingdom. Please receive this humble offering of myself. Use me as You will for the glory of the Father and the salvation of souls. Most holy Mother of God, never let me be separated from Your Divine Son. Please defend and protect me as Your Special Child. Amen.'" (July 6, 1973)

The Second Message- "Many men in this world afflict the Lord. I desire souls to console Him to soften the anger of the Heavenly Father. I wish, with my Son, for souls who will repair by their suffering and their poverty for the sinners…Prayer, penance and courageous sacrifices can soften the Father's anger." (August 3, 1973)

The Third Message- "As I told you, if men do not repent and better themselves, the Father will inflict a terrible punishment on all humanity. It will be a punishment greater than the deluge, such as one has never seen before. Fire will fall from the sky and will wipe out a great part of humanity, the good as well as the bad, sparing neither priests nor faithful. The survivors will find themselves so desolate that they will envy the dead. The only arms which will remain for you will be the Rosary and the Sign left by My Son.
Each day recite the prayers of the Rosary. With the Rosary, pray for the Pope, the bishops and priests…the Church will be full of those who accept compromises…

The thought of the loss of so many souls is the cause of my sadness. If sins increase in number and gravity, there will be no longer pardon for them. Pray very much the prayers of the Rosary.... Those who place their confidence in me will be saved."

CONCLUSION: "PRAY VERY MUCH"

In all Her visits, Mother Mary begs us to pray, pray, pray! Here are some powerful prayers we can recite daily.

The Pardon Prayer (By the Angel of Peace in Fatima)

My God, I believe, adore, hope, and love You! I ask pardon of You for those who do not believe, do not adore, do not hope, and do not love You.

Prayer to Our Lady of Medjugorje, Queen of Peace

O Mother of goodness, love, and mercy, I love you infinitely and I offer myself to you. By means of your goodness, your love, and your grace, save me. I desire to be yours. I love you infinitely and desire you to protect me.

Prayer to Our Lady of Kibeho

Blessed Virgin Mary, Mother of the Word, in your meekness, you were gracious enough to appear miraculously in Kibeho, just when our world needed it most. Grant us always the light and strength necessary to accept your call to us to be converted, to repent, and to live according to your Son's Gospel. Teach us how to pray with sincerity, and to love one another as He loved us, so that, just as you have requested, we may always be beautiful flowers diffusing their pleasant fragrance everywhere and upon everyone.

Pray to Our Lady of Garabandal (The Lady of Mount Carmel)

O Beautiful Flower of Carmel, most fruitful vine, splendor of heaven, holy and singular, who brought forth the Son of God, still ever remaining a pure virgin, assist us in our necessity! O Star of the Sea, help and protect us! Show us that you are our Mother! (pause and mention petitions)
Recite: Our Father, Hail Mary and Glory Be
Our Lady of Mount Carmel, pray for us.

Made in the USA
Middletown, DE
01 June 2024